MW00982308

The First Step

THE
FIRST STEP

MICHAEL PACEY

Carolyn Marie Souaid, Editor

Signature
EDITIONS

© 2011, Michael Pacey

All rights reserved. No part of this book may be reproduced, for any reason, by any means, without the permission of the publisher.

Cover design by Doowah Design.
Photo of Michael Pacey by Geoffrey Gammon.

"Losing the S" and "The Words" appeared in *The Antigonish Review*. "The Final Pages of Another Novel" appeared in *The Dalhousie Review*. "Lark" appeared in *Descant*. "Party" and "x,y,z" appeared in *Exile*. "Nauta, Agricola, Poeta" and "Kitchen Garden" appeared in *The Fiddlehead*. "Berry Box," "Signature," and "Invention of the Ball" appeared in *The Malahat Review*. "Catbird," "Dovetail" and "The Fatherland" appeared in *The Nashwaak Review*. "Crowbar," and "How Archimedes Made Rome Afraid" appeared in *The New Quarterly*. "Snack Foods: a Semiotics" appeared in *Prairie Fire*. "Five Mischief Pieces" was written for the 2010 edition of the Beaverbrook Art Gallery's Writing on the Wall series; each year a NB poet responds to one or more works in the Gallery's permanent collection.

This book was printed on Ancient Forest Friendly paper.
Printed and bound in Canada by Marquis Book Printing Inc.

We acknowledge the support of The Canada Council for the Arts and the Manitoba Arts Council for our publishing program.

Library and Archives Canada Cataloguing in Publication

Pacey, Michael, 1952–
      The first step / Michael Pacey.

Poems.
ISBN 978-1-897109-51-9

      I. Title.

PS8581.A22F57 2011   C811'.54   C2011-902218-4

Signature Editions
P.O. Box 206, RPO Corydon, Winnipeg, Manitoba, R3M 3S7
www.signature-editions.com

for Brian Bartlett

Contents

Crowbar

Like its name, it has a bare
simplicity, hanging from a peg
in the shed, a bar
with a beak, forged true, and
fluted to fit your hand.
Like its name, a
certain duplicity: dark,
wry, full of mischief,
a weapon if need be.
Descending from *corvus*,
the crow, a swinging span
with curved spike at its tip the Romans devised
to board enemy ships.

As tool, it's about both ends: the claw,
a pair of teeth for pulling nails,
and the business end, a thin wedge
that can pry any-
thing joined together apart.

Left behind, hanging from a peg,
like a second set of keys
to the doors, the windows,
walls, roof.
A master key
to the house's mystery: say,
in the parlour, with a crowbar.

How Archimedes Made Rome Afraid

Stopping off for water
on their way to sack Syracuse,
the Romans heard rumours
of the surprises Archimedes,
that city's famous son,
had devised for their arrival:
huge cranes to grab their warships
and drop them, bow-first in the waves;
within the gates, enormous catapults,
and mirrors arranged in parabolas
to set distant sails afire by capturing the sun.

Archimedes' artillery all in his head
(synecdoche, metonymy);
the Romans approached the locked gates,
lazily, the trickster poked
a spare board above the battlements,
waved a coil of rope; seeing these bits of
rhetoric, the peaks and gear
of huge engines of war, their shields
shook like poplar leaves. Later,
a lady's hand mirror; the troops
turn and run to their tents.

Days passed, the siege veered into torture
for those outside; sometimes,
only a child's kite or balloon
would rise above the walls,
perhaps a plume of smoke;
silk banners with a single word inscribed:
Fear   Shame   Enigma—the letters
flapping their arms in the wind, cackling.

After a week or so of this, the Romans
packed up their logical ships, and left.

Ladder

A glow in the dark garage
suspended on steel spikes—
silver—a run of rapids, encased
in ice. Set against the house,
rungs regular as chorus, an
aluminum waterfall. Origin
of the letter H, leaning on
the fruit trees, near the beginning, in
the orchard, the alphabet,
paradise.

A tool to solve walls, obstacles;
a theorem portable, its footholds
a series of assigned tasks, or
steps in an argument (if A, then
B; if B…).

Pinned to the panels
of my modest garage, a map
of the great Hegemony; and yet,
a means of rising in the world,
a one-man extension. There's
no subtracting in a ladder.
It only adds.

Hockey Stick

A spider's corner;
the garden tools no longer used:
edger, weed-spud, mattock,
half a dozen hoes…And a length of white ash
branded *Louisville Bomber*—
I haven't played hockey
in more than thirty years.

Like ox goad, or shepherd's crook, to boys
born a thousand years ago: holding the thing,
unfamiliar at first, carrying it everywhere,
a staff, a crutch, leaning on it, learning
the body of its anatomy, like a letter,
a giant-fonted J or L.   Bending the shaft,
testing it, like a Buddhist boy, given his bow.
Caressing it, learning the swing of it, a boy
with a whip, a scythe, a flail. Learning
its tricks: *snap shots, slap shots, backhands,
wristers, dekes, stick-handling.*
Shepherding the puck down the ice—shoveling
it into the corner, goading
the ox-like defencemen.
Tripping, slashing, hooking, spearing.
Ploughing into the enigmatic goalie, flailing
away, whipping the black disk at his mask.
High-sticking, butt-ending, cross-checking.
Pitchforked/horse-collared/hamstrung.
Cattle-prod/battleaxe/pike.

Nicks and cuts band the grayed shaft,
the wacky, *circa* mid-70s banana-shaped
near-boomerang blade.
Its fibreglass sheath
peeling off in long iridescent strips
like sunburn, snakeskin.

Cold mornings like this, the still-dark garage,
I'd shoulder my stick and duffel bag,
walk off into a light snow —
another soldier, heading for the front.

Berry Box

Weighing roughly the same as a moth, it wears
the jaunty manner of a straw hat,
a kite, lampshade, shuttlecock, any
construction three parts air. Blond
sheets of June poplar, slices
of summer, paper-thin like walls in Japan,
spilling off the lathe like apple peelings,
cream, scored and folded folio-wise, when
the wood's still supple, green; overlaid
crossways in pairs, to form four sides,
(a quart, quarto), four corners
that almost meet, to bale the smallest berries,
yet open to summer's breezes, so
the fruit doesn't turn, and breathes.

Kitchen Garden

Later, the garden will nourish *us*,
but in spring everything's inside out; in-
gredients, the kitchen's contents
keep seeping outside: saucers of milk
brimming with peas
that suckled overnight
before sowing at dawn;
after breakfast, bowls of honey-water
to lure slugs to sweet excess;
rosemary and sage to camouflage
the infant vegetables, table
scraps and peelings to feed
the venerable compost heap;
baking soda to erase black spot,
aspirin diluted in juice jugs
to ward off whitefly.
Last year's phone book
to be buried with ceremony
under the new peony bed;
a directory of August's blossoms.

At five when the neighbours
return home for dinner
shaking their heads, I'm still at it—
kneeling on the front walk
shaker in hand, salting
the cracks between the flagstones
where plantain and pigweed
feed.

Compost Heap (i)

A random, deliberate gathering:
last year's leaves, kitchen scraps,
weeds — peaked;
handfuls of cut stalks stacked
and interwoven, intertwined,
like the etymology of *humus*
and *human*.

Steeped in rainwater, a leaky tent
pitched behind the garage,
a backyard haycock, cornered —
the garden's true core.
Its buddha breathing calmly in
and out; forked, that
warm familiar breath
from your deft wickerwork,
o large basket stuffed, and
upended — built not to hold,
but to release.

Compost Heap (ii)

Others have written about it—
Layton, Emmanuel, Whitman—
the great Rot.
In *Timon*, the Bard terms Earth itself a heap
"that feeds and breeds by a composture."

Like children in a ring 'round a bonfire;
bending down to turn it over.

Digging deeper:
in the 11th century, Ibn al Arabi
addressed an ode to the ingredients.
A good heap should include:
"human blood, dung, lime, mortar…"
One of those long list-poems which
only ends with the author's death;
"old wool or cotton, wood ash,
street sweepings, your old poems,
old poets…"

Composing/composting: throw it all in,
then take back the indigestible bits:
stones, tree limbs. Simmer/
summer, stirring occasionally. Turning
it over. Wait
for a fine mist to rise off the peak
like an augury.
Feel for the heat with your hands.

Umbrella

Here in the dark hallway
with the scarves and jackets,
you dilate like a night-flower,
umbrella, nervous bird,
here you spread your fragile wings.

You belong to the same family
as crows and ravens: silk caprices,
the same southpaw highjinks. Spines
snapped, lying broken in ditches;
survivors arrive in mourning.

Also kin to the percussion clan,
especially the piano — the black side
of the keys — those minor tones. Taut strings
and small padded hammers —
rain's companion, and drumskin.

You smell of cloakrooms, gargoyles,
chicken bones — odours widows hoard.
Feel like patchwork bats' wings, the fingers
of tight leather gloves.

They say, once you were hoisted against the sun,
then punished with ten centuries of hail,
three of sleet.

Big hat with a handle on it!
Umbrella: dark cloud on a string;
a kite with clipped wings.

After the funeral, each home alone —
a crocodile of solitudes.

Gloves

A flock of wizened gloves
wintering over, in a grove
of bare trees by the library;
a covey, chattering,
looking for crumbs,
shaking ice from their leather wings.

A makeshift lost-and-found—
mismatched gloves impaled
on branches, pickets, hedges,
greeting the passerby with gestures
ambiguous (beckoning/warning)—
outstretched hands of the left behind,
those who drowned in snow.

Vacuum Cleaner

Still half-asleep, bumpingintothings,
the vacuum cleaner balks
at the day's first task: mucking out
its own cramped quarters;
swabbing hair, sparks, spoor
from its stall, pen, stable,
l'il room it lives in.
The maid's room.

Pets *und kinder* flee: its hysteria
sweeps the floor plan, up and
down stairs like a demonic queen, with a posse
of attendant brushes and wands.
Only powerful beings are allowed such racket,
tuned into some swarmed energy inside—
inevitable, endowed with self-locomotion
(Aristotle's category of the highest forms).
Will often feign sleep, or death—springing back
to life. Never touch its insides, shiny and
strangely warm, though it will invite you to.

Bored with your CDs? Grant them a spin
while vacuuming—you'll hear a new side,
brand new sounds, hitched to
its whined antiphony.
Say to yourself, "Boy,
this is the best stuff this guy's ever done!"

Some day they'll decode our times by
studying the contents of our vacuum bags,
like those balls of bone and fur
owls disgorge—a new archeology:
dog hair, cat vomit, insects, money,

skin, potsherds, crumbs.
What we feed our slaves.
It patrols the house
like the shadow of a tree, wicking
the corners, a slave to whims
light and haloed as dust. It creates Clean—
a kind of vacuum in the house.
Then cleans it.

Medicine Cabinet

As a child,
you long to open that door-for-gnomes;
arrange acorns and robin's eggs
on elf-sized shelves.

But the medicine cabinet's up high
like a bird house, to keep it clear of cats.

In the bathroom, where household shrines
should always be; its familiar gods female,
their images on tiny vials displayed
on slim glass ledges
that remind you of high heels.

Consulted in domestic emergencies,
like a fuse box. The Bible.

Behind a mirror, hidden
like a wall safe; babysitters, party guests
break in, root among the rolls of gauze,
ointments, pills
in search of gossip.

But it maintains the cool dignity
of a refrigerator.
A vacuum is broken when you open the door.
There's a discernible hush.

Party

(i)

At four, my parents announced
I was to have my first *party*;
even now, the word suggests
picture-book beings, magic presences.
At half-past three, the doorbell rang—
all my pals were squatting on the front steps—
"What are *they* doing here?"
I screamed.

My parents showed me their list—
"Who else would you have wished for?"

So while my guests ate gooey cake,
pulled each other's hair and
played Pin the Tail on the Jackass,
I sulked in a corner by myself,
naming the anonymous.

(ii)

We scrounged all the tubes of LePage's we could find
and hooked up at Nancy Cochrane's garage
(her parents were away).
I remember almost passing out
with the life-giving bag over my face—
then suddenly we were all dancing in a chain
around the lawnmower, chanting
"Negro music is good; yeah yeah yeah.
Negro music is good; yeah yeah yeah."
Blimp went downtown
to try to talk the hobby shops
into selling us more glue.
He never came back.

So Crow headed to campus
where he persuaded "The Bear," some shaggy guy
to sell us half a dozen hits of windowpane.
Nothing happened at first, but then
in the distance, we heard a train slowly maneuvering
into town, and someone whispered the word
shunting,
and we laughed for half an hour.

Everyone was starting to peak
when we decided to go inside—
walking into the kitchen, no one could speak—
the acid had eaten away the labels/
skinned the categories;
we had to scrounge new words
for these wonders surrounding us
(bread was *crystal-cloud,* as I recall,
apples *fire-skins,* sugar *diamond-dust*).
We sat around the dinner table till dawn
naming the anonymous.

Wasps' Nest

One of the painters, the younger, knocks
a nest of crêperie from the eaves,
and descends the scaffolding, like a boy
scrambling down with a coconut.
Stands, pensive as
Caravaggio's *David*, holding outstretched
the bearded giant's head.

Hands it to me, light
as smoky coils of cigar ash
wound into a turban.
A mummy's severed head,
swathed in dirty gray bandages.
Teacher's aide: how to dress a head wound
with newsprint sludge (how calm the man
with a hole in his head always appears).

I study the packaging, the patient
papier mâché technique; inside,
the comb's precise cells intact.

Fossil of a prehistoric melon;
a lantern composed of smoke.

Snack Foods: a Semiotics

1. *Chips*: lording your ordinariness, plodding along,
hand gloved in a faux-burlap sack, feeding
on medallions of plebeian tuber, shellacked
in vats of roiling lard: lumpengrease. Vernacular,
pulping the larval meat of the people's staple.
In Islam, they say only an animal eats in the street.
It's true, it's hard to look civilized, hard not
to look like a chimp, a chump, pinching in
the scabs and scruff at the bottom of the bag;
so, flash a churlish grin, tilt back your head and tip
a bib, a benison—salt and yellow dandruff
starching your shirt—your greasy badge.

2. *Cheesies*: abuser of the fluorescent turd,
acolyte of extruded corn,
hole rimmed with day-glo crust (puckered—
who'd kiss?) Flaunting your orange-handedness,
down at the corner store,
a trail of sunset fingerprints
on every page of *Big Jugs* magazine,
brazenly checking out sleazy videos:
Keyhole Classics, Caught from Behind, vol. 17.
Like one unashamed, caught, lips locked
round the tailpipe of a glowing, demonic machine.
And licking.

3. *Popcorn*: I'm in a movie. You're the props.
Tossing back salty manna, keyed
to my feeding: peanuts at a ballpark.
As a kid, I ran away with the circus,
never came back.
You're what we leave behind:
sawdust, droppings, empty lot.

4. *Chocolate Bar*: a tease of tissue — soon as
the money's set down — torn off; then layer
after layer your tongue unravels; you're Oblomov
at large, taking your pleasure in the streets,
self-contained, swathed in sweetness, oblivious,
hitting the core, the well-deserved fudge
— You've been a very good boy!

5. *Ice Cream Cone*: the only snack that's always cool,
au courant; the classic accessory, though it's
old-fashioned as a wide-brimmed straw hat,
or gingham. The honest wheaty grip
of the blond cone,
the melting drips of candle wax to catch,
the sweet crunch of the kick —
sunshine, long afternoons, time tapering,
contained, the light refusing to fade —
a horn, the handy cone holds all of summer.

Invention of the Ball

Soon after the wheel, but
by all but children, largely ignored.

Early models merely rolled.
And that, fitfully—
devised of hide or fur, stuffed
with grass, ashes.
No one records the first bounce,
the long parade of experiments
with pumps and patches,
a series of lags, curves, the pitch
and catch of history.

Meanwhile, back at the wheel…
mounted in sequence, a phalanx
of machinery—someone cut teeth into it:
the invention of the cog. Discs flat
and polished as coins; icons of the moon,
a cheap satellite stuck up there,
lacking all dimension, a thin dime.

Sketching engines of war
for another petty tyrant, Leonardo
paused to pen in the margin,
an alarm clock devised to rouse the dreamer,
not with bugle or thump of drum, but
by gently rubbing his feet.
This could have been a turning point.

Yet, the ball held its own. Tucked
under an arm: a map,
an assertion the earth was round.
Kids were playing ball all the while,

slapping it unceasingly
off the street's curved surface,
making it home, hum.
Chanting the old songs,
bouncing away the long afternoon.

Inkling

Hatched, an itch, twitch,
two or three particles
hook up, coalesce—
an inchling, *inkling*—brash, but
hard to define: "vague,
lacking definition" or vaguely,
"a random, deliberate gathering."

a lower-case thrash—from scratch,
wriggling in the shallows
of small dark pools; on a hunch—
mitosis, metamorphosis,
metaphorphosis—
a handful of words that begin
to circle each other slowly.

Drafts

Measled with stars, crosses, and arrows
looped and laddered, words underlined,
circled, careted in, scratched out;
check marks, coffee stains, slashes.
Shorthand terms in a shaky longhand—
a series of leaps and question marks, then
a cutting-back and sizing up,
chiseling away at the measure.

Born to the harness, like draft horses—
plodding, lead-footed, rough yet domestic,
to draw a load; their cough the dry rasp
of pencil on graph paper—
worked to bare bones, a skeleton,
driven into the ground, and abandoned.
A phase, a missing but insignificant
link. Yet somehow inclined to gambols,
gambits, odd bucks of thought
like tabletop sketches. Unabashed, and
standing in their own mistakes.

The Iconography of Photographs on Book Jackets

The author, above a tally of prizes
and previous conquests, troubled and tweedy in a jacket
worn just so slightly—bookish yet vaguely hip,
at worst elbow-patches or even (God forbid)
some kind of scarf or ascot—as with initials,
the sure sign of some kind of asshole
(i.e.: t.s., d.h., e.e., etc.).

If asked to pose for such, I'd wear
(along with my big gap-toothed NB grin)
one of those giant bibs they hand out at the House of Pies
—*that's* how I feel when I write a new poem.
Or better yet, that shot they ran in the local rag
when I snared first prize at the Hillbilly Fair,
poised in full wind-up amongst piles of oversized plush
—you can just make out the mayor
taking his turn down in the dunk-tank.
No junk, voodoo curves or wry screwballs,
everything high and hard
and a little inside.

Pencil, or Pen?

> "the quintessential *Paris Review* question"
> —George Plimpton

i. Pencil Versus

The dead write only in pencil,
faint traces on scraps of paper
they pass amongst themselves.

The feel of pencil: walking, in deep sand
into the wind, against the grain,
and very thirsty;
scratching eczema with a knitting needle.
Chalk on slate.
The smell: school (vomit, shavings, mucilage).

Some dull brute hunched over the sharpener
all afternoon, grinding well-toothed butts
to nothingness. A death rattle
of small pebbles rubbed together, gravel;
a porcupine clawing at a cabin door.

1565, the Cumberland Hills, UK:
folk find a sticky black substance
(later IDed as crystallized carbon)
underneath an uprooted tree;
start gluing stringy bits
between splinters of wood
to smear their mark on sheep.

Today, ground out of useless stubs and
stumps of scrub spruce, like
clothespins, matchsticks,
and sold by the blind for a dime.

A trail of ashes. A grey ghost
of itself, a plume of soot. Grey spelt
the English way: with a wisp
of fog. Against a winter sky, woodsmoke
slowly drifting away from the page.

Tool of tyros, deiter-minded number-
crunchers, those kept after class, their sums
rubbed out, a pink rubber nipple
to offer false hope.   A fade.

ii. Pencil Cases

Thoreau, pacing the floors
of the family pencil factory, tinkering
with the dim machines, unpacking
another load of lead from Canada.
He breathed in sawdust and graphite grit,
filled his delicate lungs with it, the mills
wearily grinding away behind him; the mills
in his head thinking outdoors, manuscripts,
even the family piano's coarsely covered
with this stuff.
Thinking TB.

"He writes with a heavy pencil," Miller, of
O'Neill. As if his work,
work of sweat, not art;
as if against the author's will,
diesel fumes rise off the page.
"There's no finesse at all;
he's the Dreiser of the stage."

Implement of hardheads, the blunt,
the dull, the overly earnest. Papa says,
"Wearing down seven #2 pencils
is a good day's work."
But after a good drink or three, you keep
breaking off points, and brooding about it,
a man who can't keep his pencil sharp,
alone in your room, the good work
not finished, the honest, homely smell
of broken pencils rebuking you,
the little slugs of lead
there on the desk.
You can fill in the rest.

iii Pen: a Paean

Dip into the blue/black ocean of ink
and just like that, you're *off*...(all writing is
travel writing). Swept along the holy river,
"a black river of ink," as Cocteau puts it:
"I commence to write above my head,
in bed with a Bic, as a fly walks on the ceiling."
Effortless, the slide, silent glide as you roll along,
the wet dye hugs the paper, is dry.

No blots, as in the past,
when ink spilled prodigal
from quills, inkwells,
fountain pens. And fast as words can fly.

Almost all agree: the ballpoint's
the pinnacle.
Atwood: "I prefer to write with a pen.
My handwriting's fast."
Hughes: "What tools do I require? Just a pen."
Bishop: "For poetry, I use a pen."
Jane Graham: "I don't much like the *feel* of pencil."

Cartridges, reservoirs
that tap into oceans,
deep currents of blue/black ink;
okay, at first, only a somewhat less
primitive page-scratching device, but
the modern began
with ballpoint's invention:

The Biro brothers, Laszlo and Georg,
on a lazy summer afternoon
on a beach in 1935 Hungary,
following a ball that skips and skims
with brio, over the waves —

and there it is,
birth of the rolling word,
silent and wet, above the waters,
wriggling on the page. The key:
a way to keep ink
from blotting and smudging,
a ball
that wicks, inks itself, and rolls it right
onto paper. Where it sticks, insta-set.

Quick as a fox, jumping over the lazy dog,
quick as thought, quick as a ball
at play in its socket, orbiting around and
bouncing over the blue legible world.

Eraser

A pencil's a candle burning at both ends—
waxing/waning; writing/erasing.
Scribbling = lots of scrubbing out;
vide Nabokov: "My pencils outlast their erasers."

Sullen, ambiguous substance; opaque
as ambergris. Dense as Neptune.
Amnesia. Slices of forgetfulness.

Nipple-shaped & dyed bubblegum-pink:
schoolday soothies for slow weaners. Switched
in junior high for gritty, snub-nosed blocks & wedges
of tough, rubbery brain-stuff.
Learn slow burn of the manual delete: stubborn floor-
scouring frictioning of words and skin
from paper, a snail-like procession.
Slow:
because it's much easier to say something
than to take it back.
To get milk from trees.

Erasure: the act itself. Also, the words erased.
And a third: the mark left behind: scar, welt,
blurred skid, dirt. That scorched earth look—
not smoke. Smoked.
Because even in pencil, you never erase
that trail of mistakes, hounding behind you.

If only you *could* turn them into
a pile of rubbery crumbs
to be whisked away, with the back of your hand.

Typewriter

I'd approach the black box (labeled *Olympia*)
in a solemn manner, wearing my magic pyjamas.
It slept in my father's den: even opening
the box (what would fly out?) a kind of sin.
Quietly, I'd take the thing from its cage,
try teaching it to sing.

Tapped out strings of consonants, snakeheads
fanging the page, oozing from my fingertips.
But putting words together—
mired in birdbrained hunt & peck—
I suspected it wasn't lack of speed,
mastery, that made writing rote, mechanical.
Inside, its guts all levers, braces, springs.
What I wanted was more like pressing a key
and a certain note would play.

Eventually I'm smashing both hands down,
trying to hit all the keys at once,
get it all out. A lump of metal: 26 characters
jammedtogether, welded fast as wire braces.
Prying them apart with a letter opener,
butter knife, tweezers—its tongue
flopping around on the carpet,
spools on floor; ink
fingers, thumbsmeared paper.

Get everything back in the box
before he comes home. But first,
something to wrench these letters
apart—a crowbar—or better,
bomb, to blow up this dumb old machine,
alphabet.

x, y, & z

Recently all my thoughts alphabetical
center on *x*, *y*, & *z*: the vestigial stump,
the scruff, the ruins,
the wreckage of the alphabet,
or as Nabokov said, the zoo.
Antipode to those clean-cut poster boys,
the ABCs, these aren't your A-type personalities,
chain-smoking characters
panhandling in front of the liquor store,
plonking away on their zithers & xylophones;
loitering outside darkened train stations
as you glide by in the night —
from now on, all the signposts you pass
will be in cyrillic.

x — mark of the illiterate, the unletter,
the scrawl. Marx, Nixon, Hendrix,
(don't trust anyone with an x in their name);
— the unknown, the x-factor, the x-ray
(because its inventor didn't know
what force he was working with).
x marks the spot; tripled — keep away;
in sequence — to cancel or obliterate.
Yet, the power to magnify, multiply. Xerox.

y — the alphabet's androgyny;
some nights, when the moon's full,
goes about as a vowel. Some kind of
yin yang, y/x/y chromosome's
in the equation, in the stew now.
A yoking (yolking?) of signs,
of signifiers (zeugma?),
sandwiched between those
gargoyles, x & z.

z — a slash. A zigzag. The anti-letter.
The zenith. The zone. Zero
to zillions. A to Z; say it out loud,
and right away the inevitable questions
raise their pointy heads.
Riddles resolved? All's revealed—lit up
by a succession of lightning-shaped z's?
(The zebra did it.) Or more like,
z as in snooze, the big vacation, some excellent *zzzzz*
ad infinitum, replicating themselves right off the edge of the
page.

A final word? It's right here, *zymurgy*—
the study of fermentation;
this one ends up in a yeasty bog,
a noxious ooze.

Q

Q ventures out infrequently;
he feels others' eyes on him like
a fusillade of fish hooks.
On his… plume.

You might come upon him late at night,
alone under the snow of stars, propped
against it like a tripod,
scanning the dome for comets.

Born of O, but with this appendage
to mark him apart: dragging in the dust,
pinched in shut windows and doors,
rippling in pique, switching back and
forth in tune with the radio. Or erect,
testing the air as he defecates.
Each day becomes a Quest.

In secret of course, it affords *some* pleasure:
at night in his room, lips pursed,
he combs his brush out slowly, taking off
its bristled stiffness
in the strands of its long double-curve.

Sometimes he *must* slip out—he's run
out of Quince—a brisk stroll to the corner…
But children, the little monkeys, invariably
spot him, and pad up behind and
take their turn.
Quietly, step on his tail.

@

Conceived, 6th C: scribes
cutting corners, wind d round
a for *ad* (L: at, towards).

Version b: born in 16th C
Venetian counting houses
short for *amphora* (a measuring device).

Lingered on, in bookkeepers'
ledgers: *at the rate of.*
Like hidden interest.

Then, '71; re-conceived as hub
or pivot in first e-mail address
(between user ID & PC).
Now, supernova.

With no global name: France & Italy
call it the snail; Norwegians, pig's tail;
Germans, monkey's tail;
Chinese, little mouse.
A dog in Russia,
Finns see a sleeping cat.

All focus on *at*; the fixed, at rest,
self-nested aspect; its new mode,
myth, needs more *towards*:
a head with arrow whirling out,
the lightning thoughts of a god; that spark,
that *whoosh* of a message successfully sent—
what else can @ be called but apollo?

Losing the "S"

A few more disappear each day—
the names of people who say hello
on her walk (*Sharon, Sasha*);
the names of flowers in her yard
"What are those small bells, at the edge
of the gully, I have too many of?"
Solomon's Seal
And those blooms everywhere
in so many different shades?
Sweet Rocket
Speculates, at 88, she's used up
her allotment of that overused letter,
the "S" section of her brain worn away.

Guiding her around the garden at dusk,
I tell her as consolation,
it's better this way maybe—
the familiar blooms in their familiar beds,
but then, every so often
coming upon blossoms anonymous—
their scent mixed with a sibilant hiss,
a ghostly "S" suspended in the air,
regal, unspoken.

At the Owl's Nest

They're anonymous, passing the flock
of small clay owls in the doorway
with their boxes and bundles;
all winter, someone had been piecing off
their Nabokov: *Pale Fire, Glory, Ada,*
and then in the last cruel days of March
I discovered with a sigh
the long-sought *Speak, Memory.*
I pictured someone (elderly?) struggling
through the drifts, the hardbound volumes
in plastic shopping bags, as some wag said,
the accessories of the poor.
Up the three flights to the small shop,
his disintegrating library
(like the well-worn furniture
turned into February firewood)
weighed on the scales
and exchanged, no doubt, for little more
than a foxed Frank Yerby,
or a well-worn Frank Slaughter.

Paying for my latest find, I asked
who brought in all the Nabokov;
my only reply—an arched brow
and my chattering change.
But soon I started getting messages,
clues, stuffed in my mailbox:
a waterlogged copy of *Great Expectations;*
chapters ripped from an old edition
of *Pilgrim's Progress;* pieces from jigsaw puzzles
began appearing in my backyard—
a handful more every day—scraps of trees or sky,
then a bit of ribbon and a girl's hair,
the corner of her eye.

In spring the code ceased,
but simultaneously an unexpected harvest
started at the Owl's Nest—one by one
the Singer I'd been longing for:
Shosha, Passions, The Magician of Lublin.
All through April and May
I skipped up and down the three flights, well, singing.

The Words

Each evening alone with the dictionary,
I'd cache in long columns
a tinker's vocabulary—nouns, verbs, adjectives—
the words I planned to use in my poems:
vase, veil, verandah, vial,
violet, vocabulary, vowel...

Letter by letter (the easy ones first:
q, x y z, then *v),* late into the night,
I worked my way through the alphabet,
hoarding the snug, the euphonious, the spare:
hoard, hobble, home, honeycomb,
huddle, hunch, husk...

I knew that to a poet's fingertips
words were emblems in braille; reaching out,
they tuned in/turned up/struck hidden terms
the way others witch water, or jewels:
echo, eclipse, effigy, emblem,
emerald, envelope, essence...

My first fumbling, cut & paste poems, proceeding
as if words were just beads on a necklace strung:
name, necklace, nectar, nest,
nexus, nib, nomenclature...
I didn't know it would take the words so long
to work their ink beneath my skin.

Signature

We were learning about cheques, one afternoon
in Junior Finance—writing our name for money.
Mr Phalen told us to perfect our signature
and practise it repeatedly, until it was set
like cement, minted
as a medium of exchange.

I looked around: the boys were devising
shark-headed loops and swaggered tails
such as titans of high finance might jot,
or gigolos, jagged griffonage all style;
the girls were curling their vowels and consonants
resignedly, making them a little more pretty.

I have a child's autograph, circa grade three,
the year I half-mastered the cursive,
couldn't change my scrawl then, or now;
like most left-handers, doggedly constructing
my little snare upside down,
a damp smear befouled, as afterthought,
by my own hand anyhow.

So I just sat there for the hour, staring
out the window, the teacher droning on
about stubs, balances, fraud,
the spring sun making puddles in the yard,
my classmates at their desks in orderly rows,
bent upon their forgeries,
signing themselves in, over and over.

For Anna Blauveldt

I read of your father's death
in last week's cathedral newsletter;
the dean said, "Yes, of course
she'll be here for the funeral;
she's flying in from Reykjavik tomorrow...
Didn't you know?
She's Ambassador to Iceland now."

We sat beside each other in junior high:
the golden sheaves of your gathered hair,
and those upland meadows—
o the blue fields of your blouses!

I read in a newspaper article once,
more books by Canadian authors
are bought in Reykjavik
than in all of Ontario.

I see you sitting on a rock
beside the sea, reading,
in a field of small bell-shaped flowers,
Icelandic poppies perhaps. Ice floes
sail by slowly
while you read on, near Reykjavik;
your blue eyes the tiny flags
of a country we heard rumours of,
but never traveled to, together

Nauta, Agricola, Poeta

In Caesar's day all nouns pertaining to profession
marshaled masculine declensions
except three, to which feminine inflections
were appended: nauta, agricola, poeta.

Sailors, one suspects were *always* suspect—
all those nights alone with the stars
and a bunch of swell guys;
the way they sway when they walk.
And their hair and clothes forever scented
with brine from the source,
what Joyce called "that sunken cunt, the sea."

But *farmers..?* Unless again it's gender by proxy,
proximity: they're fastened to Mother Earth.
That's it—farmers are the ultimate mama's boys,
out there in the barn, always hanging up their
tools dutifully on the appropriate peg.
Don't forget Hesiod's advice: "Ploughing, a man
should plant his foot as softly as a maiden."

The poet needs no explanation: one almost *expects*
one's literary pals to lean over and proclaim
their pansexuality, to assume gayness
as a gift or a mask or a crown.
Kundera said "A poet's a man who *loves* his mom."
Think of Rilke, reared in silks.
Or a boy who eavesdrops, mimics, mocks,
sucks his thumb, makes lists,
snoops through medicine cabinets and
underwear drawers, at home with
and mollycoddled cunningly
in his mother tongue.

Reading Proust

Oh, those interminable evenings at the de Guermantes!
Dragging myself to another one of your do's,
awake half the night, week after week, in bed
in uncomfortable formal wear, while you spout some
mumbo-jumbo to your phoney-moroney friends;
those interminable snake-like sentences.
Talk about lost time!

How did you ever hook up
with such a pack of counterfeits?
How about bowing out, taking a rain check,
say you're not well (well, you're *not*).
No wonder when you and Joyce met,
neither could think of anything to say.
Doesn't the odd, interesting person
ever drop by these soirées, just by mistake?
Did you ever consider volunteering,
once a week, at an orphanage?
Didn't you ever meet anyone *nice*?

The volumes stacked before me like an obelisk;
the volume's what I *really* want to talk about it:
instead of repeating the repetitive,
why not *suggest*? As is, I have to keep
looking at my watch; began speed-reading post-Swann,
just skimming, as we dodder to the abyss.
Did you try writing a précis first?
Did you ever try writing a poem?

Hurl

I vomited all over Europe;
the nauseous generation, kids dragged across
the Continent and back, carsick and sulking
in the back seats of '60s station wagons,
kids posed for photographs
beside some classical statuary,
doubled over and retching in a ditch,
barfing with castles, cathedrals in the distance,
stacking our own little impromptu shrines
along the tourist route, our stomachs somersaulting
through hairpin curves high up in the Alps—
sometimes there was no place to stop,
so just roll down the window and let 'er rip
(Dad had to hose down the Ford every 100 k's).
The natives slowing down, honking,
making suggestions with their colourful gestures—
"another uncouth North American,"
they'd offer in their musical tongues;
as if bending over and spewing bolus
on their homeland, some kind of critique or stance.

Which on some level, of course, it was:
the offal masquerading as food
(Hey! Where's the pizza and fries?),
the pockmarked roads, the carcasses proudly
displayed in every crummy little village,
the Temples of Gore
masquerading as art galleries:
saints bound, burned, bludgeoned,
one guy with a quiver's worth
of arrows up his ass, the *de rigeur* restagings
of the hog-tied Christ, always that same look
on his face—"I'm gonna puke"
(cousin even to the carsick). A torment
unending: upchucking at checkpoints,

losing my lunch as we lose our way,
throwing up on the map, little chunks as tiny countries,
bringing it all up, tossing it off, honking, hurling,
rolfing, purging — saying in the basest terms of any esperanto,
any universal language, "I can't swallow this."
I threw up all over Europe.

Chuck Berry's Aroma Diary
(*New Yorker* 21/1/02)

Still duckwalking the continent at 80,
Chuck catches the day's odours in his journal,
uncanned Americana you'll never find by looking—
now every landscape's on tape, loud and invasive,
take it or leave it (if you don't want to watch it,
just gouge out your eyes).
But the nose takes on the world
one whiff at a time, stubbornly, stays tuned
to the pure particular:
the scent of burning oak leaves
in October in Missouri;
an oncoming breeze
laden with the smell of mint plants…

Sitting up beside the driver
in his signature sailor's cap,
eyes and ears closed to traffic,
Chuck gesticulates, as if conducting
aroma symphonies (roll over, Walt Whitman);
lays it all down in his motel room
later that night:
a passing pipe smoker
using rum-and-maple tobacco;
the uncontaminated breasts
of a female companion…

He's sniffed out the motherlode right here,
a hoard of ur-odours, ur-flavours;
the intangible tang; he's turned his back,
his beak, on the Old World,
as on the cheap stink of patchouli
or eau de cologne:
France has the worst restaurants—
scrawny chickens in their windows.

My dad used to grow vegetables,
cucumbers, squash, tomatoes —
the vegetables in Europe don't compare...

It's here — the plants, the scents,
spring up puckish and boyish and fresh;
it's here — the odour of conifers
explorers inscribed in their chronicles
long before they sighted land,
still hanging in the air like resin.
It's here — the fragrance of young women
turning their bodies for the sun's tongue,
the bouquet of cattle burning around the clock,
the interior of a new automobile
I just purchased, and although
I detest the smell of alcohol,
somehow I'm carried asunder
by the surprise of liquor
on the breath of a strange lady...

The Overbook

Researchers in the media lab at MIT
have perfected the last book, the *Overbook*.
Written in electronic ink on black and white spheres
which flip on and off, like fish scales,
waves in the sun,
it can form the printed pages of any book scanned,
with the push of a few buttons on the spine.

They've entered the Library of Congress
(20 million volumes) — and now scan the globe
for other texts, other tongues.

But that won't be enough.
They'll decide to encode all *possible* novels, poems,
plays etc., with obvious restrictions
of vocabulary, syntax etc.,
so we can access everything now.

And that won't be THE END, either…
Some pixel-imps, hacker/bards will chew away
at the ragged margins of the *Overbook* —
screw up the codes, turn text
on itself, enact strange new poetics.
Make the *Uberbook* one big mess.

Or else, the wires will run out of juice, computers
everywhere junked, in ruin.
There won't be any books, superfluous,
burned for fuel.

But somebody will pick up a piece of slate, birchbark,
skin, and not because there's much to say, because
he can't help himself — start
the story rolling again;
his hand a hungry mouse, scratching away.

The First Step

*After his execution, Saint Denis picked up his head and
walked home from Montmartre to the town which bears
his name, several miles north of Paris. Hearing of his feat,
salon celebrity Mme. du Duffand remarked, "The first step
is the hardest."*

It rolls…then settles in the basket,
just another wrinkled cabbage;
you stoop to retrieve your head
like an errant hat, somewhat gingerly
grab it by the hair, the handles of a purse,
or no, less personal, something
you were asked to fetch at the store,
late shopper reluctantly settling for
the last wilted head of lettuce, or
heavier: a turnip
for that chatterbox, the
all-important ball of meat.

Swing it like a parcel
picked up at the post office, an empty pail of paint,
a bucket of water it's okay to spill.
Eventually, your hair cuts into your hands,
leaves marks. But for now, gathered together,
in one handy bag,
all that baggage we drag around with us,
all the old garbage.
(Many long for
that long walk to the store;
abandon husband, wife, head.)

Before you set off, the inevitable pause:
a crevasse opens up at your feet.
Doubt.
No one would deny nowadays,

that those who've lost their head
learn to depend on other senses.
But, even so heightened,
how does one *go on*, let alone
find the way home?

Faith
knows the world's real, not abstract.
Or is it your feet?
Poke one forward, toddlerwise, from scratch,
then ditto the mate: the first step's
a piece of sky, and then the next. The first step's
like reaching the ladder's last rung, and,
finding it doesn't go far enough,
you kick it away, walk out into thin air.
Find purchase there.

Your feet (the body's loyal peasants)
can almost smell their way home;
as for hearing, ears are overrated;
the whole body is always listening (not just
legs and feet, like spiders, either).
Our nerves form a fierce tree.
Bones, even the tiniest,
hear vibrations in earth, the air;
hear rain, thunder and music.

Two thousand steps to make a mile;
forty-two bones and twenty-one muscles
to take a step;
each bone points, each muscle
pulls me out of the city.

Smell and taste are the same,
outside the head; the scents and nectar
of wildflowers identical, translated
by my breathing skin.

My muscles guide and balance me,
especially, the vast and wing-like muscles
in the back, *lattissimus dorsa.*

Do you really think your hands can't read
the difference between an orange
and a pear? That it's not
your whole body that tastes a peach?
Your body deaf and blind to the world?
That it wouldn't, right away,
fall into its own cadence, the way
it remembers music, perfectly?
Or recognize roadside scenes as old friends?

Homing in now, the way trout return
to a particular stream, the taste of
a certain ratio of common plants
by the water's edge, or more,
the way their combination blends
with local mud and clay.

Dark when I arrive; ken to every stone
I kick the last kilometre;
the village walks out to meet me,
bearing my name as its own.

The last one hundred steps, sheep bells
and smells from the fields
hold me for a moment, holding my breath,
holding my blind head outstretched
like a lantern.

Rain and Sleep

1.   There are so many things about rain
        I know only when I'm asleep.

2.   The air becomes charged—
        just before the switch, you can taste it—
        the leaves turn their white undersides up,
        eyes roll back, a different current
        begins to flow.

3.   Rain comes like sleep—a lilted whisper.
        Sleep descends like rain upon mown grass.

4.   Reading a long novel—a series of naps
        between chapters; a series
        of brief showers in the yard.

5.   drizzling   drowsing
        dowsing   dozing
        sleet   sleep

6.   The sound of rain—you long for sleep.
        In dreams, you walk remembered streets,
        holding an umbrella.

7.   That woman you seek, but
        never find—she's rain;
        she's sleep.

Sorrow's Army

Goths wake at three, already weary.
Put black beetles
they find in the bathtub
into a cereal bowl, crush
them into mascara.

Scowl in the mirror.

White moths on their closet floor
are reborn
on their porcelain cheeks.
Inside, a wardrobe arrayed in 17
shades of black, from midnight
to mortimer.

Emerge as the sun
melodramatically expires.
Petulantly lick an ice cream cone
for dinner, then
skulk the streets,
oddly drawn to porch lights.

Home. They look
in the closet once more;
there's always something missing—
a shade they can never find, the only
one missing from the set
something blacker than black itself.

Burrs

1. Like one knitting by the fire in a book,
    I sit by the hour, winnowing burrs
    from the spaniel's silky fur,
    the occupation of a total fool.

2. Patiently he waits, wearing his shirt of fire,
    as his master's hands
    work through the knots and whorls of hair
    until baring and seizing the root,
    (tensed, he relaxes now)
    the irritant: houndstooth, burdock
    or cockleburr; the rub, the nub,
    the pearl.

3. Autumn, 1948:
    George de Mestral, Alpine mountaineer,
    plucking burrs from his lederhosen
    and from Victor, his devoted Saint Bernard
    pricks his finger — sees suddenly
    a nuisance inside out: fasteners devised
    of thousands of interlocking hooks
    and eyes. Christens his brainchild
    Velcro (the name stuck), for velvet,
    his favorite English word,
    and crochet, French for hook.
    Likewise entertained,
    I think only about burrs,
    autumn's obsession with spreading the word.

4. *Burdock*: spiked mace-head punky
    as pincushion-stuff; burning orb
    hurled at passersby; ball of gall
    (to be removed entire,
    or, bract burst, wrestle

with a swarm of stinging barbs).
A globe of won't-let-go,
enarmoured as porcupine
or hedgehog in fright.

Cockleburr: also girded with hooks
but egg-shaped, and harder,
as if constructed of steel and wood;
placed under the medieval subject's tongue—
a device to extract the truth.

Beggar's Tick (also known as
hound's tooth, or stick-tight):
clinging, tongue-shaped
double-pincered parasite
hanging, thick as scales
or coat-of-mail.
It punctures the skin
and works its way to the brain.

5.   Shklovsky said every poem
should contain several knots or burrs—
rough patches, irregularities,
snarls of words to entangle
the reader, "to make the familiar difficult,
to increase the difficulty
and length of perception…
to make the stone stony."

To make the burr burrish…
Hitchhiking hellspoor!
Barbed hagride!
Plague of egg-laden leeches.
Bête noire of the dog-walking set.
Pods!

6. *Burr,* from *burst,* Old High German for bristle:
    a rough or prickly envelope of a fruit;
    a small rotary cutting tool;
    a bit on a dentist's drill;
    a trilled uvular *r*;
    a rough humming sound;
    to make a whirring sound.

   Burrer: 1. one who removes burrs
   from sheep, which greatly devalue the wool.
                    2. A dim-witted fellow.

7. *Burrer's strategies:* unwind it slowly,
    patiently, let it play like a trout;
    don't fight against
    the set of the barbs,
    they'll only burrow deeper
    like fish hooks or quills.
    Allow it to work itself free
    willingly, unwillingly.
    It must come out
    the way it went in.

8. The definition of a *fool:*
    one who, resident of a burr-infested region
    (like New Brunswick)
    agrees to groom
    a Cavalier King Charles spaniel.

   Back from a run at the river's edge,
   my spaniel's ringlets entangled,
   ensnared from ruff to plume,
   I kneel to the task once again—
   sifting through the chaff:
   leaves, maple keys, tufts of lichen
   like steel wool, spruce gum,
   sticky butternut stems. To get to the nub.

A dog built like a broom,
animated mophead
with train of leaves, an entourage
of burrs. A dog devised
to warm a monarch's lap,
to strut about a manicured landscape
by Sir Joshua Reynolds,
harassing the peacocks.

Five Mischief Pieces
   for Gordon Dunphy

1. Touch Bowl

A small wooden bowl, snack-sized,
nut-brown, like one set down beside you
at a party—a salt-lick—irrevocable, your hand
back and forth. Others join in, hands swoop/
skim, glance/graze, the air full of whoops and
squawks—the tiny bowl's surrounded now,
near empty: birds at a feeder…

But this bowl's just for touch; bowl
spared the burden of content.
A harbour for our hands. Bachelard says,
"Everything round invites a caress." Wood
especially longs for touch: our deep-rooted
kinship fleshed. So we stroke curves, fondle
lustre, rub swirls of grain until
this fat brim's rimmed with salt, prints;
our sweat seeps into its pores.
Bowl as unending fullness.

Here in the Gallery, where signs say
Do Not Touch Do Not Touch *Please*
Do Not Touch, a small wooden bowl whispers
touch touch touch.

2. Burl Platter

On his lathe (driveshaft of an old Chevy)
Gordon spins golden urns, bowls, platters
from burls: benign tumours on trees.
Inside, cells crazed, the grain spirals figurative:
everyday *bird's-eye*, but also: *bee's wing,*
bear scratches, moonshine, fiddleback…

A palette, a piquant meal of shimmering
*salmon tail*s and plump *buttered shrimp*
on a bed of dimpled *peanut shells*
and *grains of rice,* one saucy *tiger stripe*
curled at the rim — enough for a feast.
Handed to us on a platter.

3. Fungus Spoon

Spoon with a long generous bowl,
a long, almost a ladle's handle; communal
spoon slipping easy over lips and tongue,
the way its wooden bowl and your mouth
spoon together. Let the soft tissues decide
between this weathered old friend and
metal knife or fork.

An inlay of green fungus forks its way
across the lip to lend a funky tang
to soup or stew; a knife-edge that rivers
through the yellow birch, a spongy
tongue licking, flickering, spider-fingering
its way through the wood, a row of green
teeth gnawing away at their host.
That many-branched vein of mischief
that runs through his work. One more
large spoonful of what we need —
strong medicine.

4. Cherry Vessel

Vessels possess a certain gravity,
a solemn quality. From ancient days,
burdened with life-giving wine or water.
Unmoved by wrath or mercy,
they travel on, inviolate.

Gordon's vessels contain cracks and holes,
so they'll breathe; give and take, like trees,
over centuries. Punctures, scars —
wear them as ornaments.
Like a coat inside out, slung on a chair
for mending — its viscera: the clenched lips
of rough seams, guts of pockets —
jewels.

Blood of rubies, wine-dark, see
its veins, the red stain of itself exploding
in spalting lines that bend down low.
It slakes our thirst, this vessel of mercy.

5. Inlaid Urn

Vein of mischief that runs through... inside
cells crazed, the grain spirals figurative...
You choose the wood prudently, before
turning your own urn; wood that speaks
to you. No longer that desire
to talk back.

Gouge and skew, the flesh
shearing away in long curls and shavings.
Shape it, until the two of you hold.
Weeks of polishing...then one day,
a sounding: bend down low, your mouth
against its broad lip, you sing.

He fondled the five small squares of wood
until they shone like treasure,
framed them with resin and
set them in place:
olive to bring peace to his sleep,
purpleheart for courage,
mahogany's ruby fire for warmth;

ebony's shine, to fill the dark with envy.
And *lingnum vitae*, his emblem,
the Tree of Life.

Wood in his hair, eyes, lungs
(where the fungus works away),
he made a mouth, an opening
just big enough to wriggle in,
through three hundred hoops.
Inlaid. His destination inevitable:
he climbed inside a tree.

Dear Claude
for Claude Liman

Received your letter of August 28th:
"the moose got in my way (or I in his)
a week ago last night;"
the envelope stuffed with gory "after" photographs:
fuzzy testicles suspended from the rear-view mirror,
a rack of antlers in the passenger seat;
"See the bag of moose entrails
hanging in the back of my car;
see me by the side of the road
holding a passing farmer's hoe,
pouring moose shit from my loafers!"
I once praised your poems by saying how I envied your gift
for getting *inside* things; months later you admitted
you were still wondering what I meant by that,
and what *did* I mean by that anyway?
And then I had to admit that though I knew it was true,
I didn't know exactly what I meant myself—
could only give examples of your lines as evidence.
"My journals and I lived through the experience,
although the sickly-sweet smell of moose shit still clings to me."
But this journey into the grotesque—what is that,
a spleen or liver wrapped around the spokes
of your bicycle back in the hatchback?
This is not what I meant.
Pioneer Yankee poet, riding the marginal
Ontario highways, pointed North,
writing off your blood-red Integra
jousting with this lord of the forest.
Certainly puts your delicate lyric
about squashing the neighbour's cat
in perspective, doesn't it?
"See me in my American Gothic pose
with wrecked car and hoe instead of pitchfork...
I'm mighty glad to be alive, old buddy."

Did you have time to hit the horn as it bellowed
and you collided/collaged/merged?
Time to murmur Thoreau's last words—
"Moose, moose?" Time to stare into its eyes?
Or did you merely brace yourself and begin
to bare the inner workings of the wild?

Decoding the Dance
(*Karl von Frisch, 1886–1982*)

Even before I went to school,
I had a little zoo in my room;
a pet woodpecker's
tattoo on the drainpipe
wakens Karl for breakfast at *Brunnwinkl,*
on the shores of *Lake Wolfgang,*
where waves speak and trees chatter,
birds chant and hills echo —
a boyhood talking book.
Their dialogue ongoing, wide-ranging,
but above all *to be* = bees:
Many a time in later years
a walk planned for a day
ended after a few hundred yards
in front of a bees' nest —
I couldn't tear myself away.

His first coup at Munich U:
fish *can* hear, are always listening,
in fact (of the major composers),
they prefer Mozart.
We had to put up notices everywhere,
even in the cloak room, saying
"No whistling, please. No singing."
Minnows in winter
and bees in summer, I have not so far
run out of problems to investigate…
Always another bee in his bonnet:
next, swatted that insult to insects —
that flowery language
is an indecipherable scrawl
before their "colour-blind" eyes;
verified the inverse, the obvious:
the bright petals are, in fact,

colourful inn signs
announcing where nectar's to be had.

He submerges himself in his work
as in a sticky honeypot;
on the go while the sun shines,
busy as a professor:
I sometimes trained my bees
at four different places at once,
rushing around from one to the next
the whole day long …
During the long winter of the Great War,
alone in his waxlit cell
constructing transparent hives;
trying to climb right inside the combs,
their lexicon, their swarm of grammar.
Trying to crack the code
buzzing in his head,
like a radio muttering in another room—
he can't quite make out the words.
It was clear to me that the bee community
possessed an excellent intelligence service,
but where was the text?
This gave me no rest…

Every summer as soon as term ends,
Karl flies back home to the hives,
buttonholing friends and family
for his beeing-bees, bee-ins:
After I'd marked a visitor with paint,
I'd signal its departure
to my brother Hans, posted on a hilltop,
by a blast on an old cow horn,
a primitive instrument much treasured
by our colony.
He'd then alert Deiter by ringing a cowbell,
and Deiter passed on the message

by means of a trumpet signal
to the observers at Brunnwinkl…
Never before or since have I
blown into a cow horn with such fervour!

April 19, 1919. The first breakthrough.
On a clear morning, a path to a clearing.
9 a.m.; as soon as all was quiet,
Karl filled a dish with sugar water,
and set it down;
watched a scout discover it,
then return to the hive.
I could scarcely believe my eyes.
She performed a round dance on the comb,
which greatly aroused the foragers
around her, and induced them to fly back
to the feeding place. This, I believe,
was the most far-reaching observation of my life.
Round Dance: set down small
circles, encoding closeness;
then move on to other points
on the dance-floor, drawing small
circles, feeding particles of nectar
to the onlookers; *here*, the dancer
says, passing around the music,
the message, the beat, *it's right here.*
Give them the buzz.

Was it conceivable that their language
should have a word for "distance"?
A signal to indicate "direction"?
This seemed all too fantastic to be true.

August 2, 1944: Karl sets out
dishes containing sugar water
scented with lavender —

small dishes near the hive,
a large one a fair distance away:
to my intense surprise the blue bees
from the nearby feeding-place
danced the round dance,
and the red bees all performed
a new dance, a tail-wagging dance.

Tail-Wagging Dance: set out a
figure eight on the floor; the sign
suggesting distance,
the endless shape of flight.
Before beginning the second loop,
pause, and wag
that abdomen, suggestive of booty,
wag it from side to side;
the cadence metes out the reach,
the measure, the feet.
Two blocks away's a jitterbug jump,
a mile's more like the *Blue Danube*.
Now pick up that second loop
and pull it through;
start your second eight
but don't forget to pause,
hold the beat, and give that butt
a shake; *here it is*—to and fro—
here's where the honey hides.

I remember the hour: it was midday
on June 15, 1945, when I realized
that marked dancers
which had collected nectar
400 yards due north
performed their wagging run
straight down on the vertical comb,
whereas unmarked bees danced
in all possible directions.

On the vertical surface of the hive
the dancer encodes the sun—
translates its position with
the angle of her line of flight
to an angle with the force of gravity.

Following a sudden impulse of curiosity,
I turned one of the combs
covered with dancing bees in my hand
horizontally—and spun it round and
round like a turntable—
the bees adjusted to the right direction
like the needle of a compass.

Karl kept refining the syntax—
discovered, for example, that the figure
eight for distance is figurative,
never a literal beeline, but figures in
headwinds, detours, obstacles, etc.
My chief concern was to discover, if possible,
any further words in the bees' language;
say, to go "up" or "down." Scouting
the ruins of Munich right after the war,
scaling the tallest bombed-out houses
and crippled chimneys,
with dishes of lavender water.

In the fifties, Karl roams the globe—
a series of tours across America:
the flickering cinema of the bees
already dances on the screen
as he appears on stage, garbed
in the robes of a Minoan bee priest,
intoning into a microphone,
The dance of the bees can never
be conveyed by words alone;
the audience is rapt, reading

the words of the bees, as Karl drones on:
Bees are as old as the hills.
This may be one of the reasons
they appear to be so mature,
so perfect in many ways.
Footage from his study tours—Ceylon,
Brazil, India—appears on the screen;
he's compiling a "comparative philology"
of the language of bees (supplied
with honey by the Rockefellers).
Now the camera pans to odd-shaped combs,
a diversity of bees being introduced,
then dancing for each other:
Though the rhythmic pattern
of their dance is slightly different,
American bees can understand
European bees without difficulty.

Cries of Birds

The best books are read
till dawn crawls in —
cries of birds scissor the text,
dark wings/words tilt and
swerve, fly off;
their first songs bleed
through, merge.
Cardinals and vireos wake
as I swirl towards sleep.

One morning, Virginia Woolf heard
the birds
speak to her in ancient Greek.
Their calls burr inside my head,
beaks making a music before
words. Favourite books, I've
set aside, and heard the singing of birds.

The Bard's Birds

Their coming was the result of one man's fancy.
That man was Eugene Schieffelin, a wealthy New
York drug manufacturer. His curious hobby was
the introduction into America of all the birds
mentioned in Shakespeare. —Edwin Way Teale

A dozen or so, whistling and clacking,
work the turf of my lawn,
all offspring of a single line—
"I'll have a starling shall be taught to speak"
(*1 Henry IV* I.iii; 1. 224).
Would that Will had blotted that bird,
careted in *paraquito* or *crow* instead.
1891. It's Saturday; Eugene drives
his carriage into town, to see his brood safely ashore
from the Southampton liner.
Takes the large wire cage to Central Park;
a group of small boys playing hackysack
pause to watch as he lifts the latch—
cackling, a hundred greasy starlings
fly up into the trees. Within ten years
they've colonized the city,
and struck out across the continent.

The brother of a friend became obsessed with *Lear*
several years ago—purchased videos
of every performance ever filmed,
black and white, silent, puppet;
sent to Japan for an anime version,
finally, spent months on the Internet
tracking down the elusive claymation *King Lear.*
Omnivorous, the Bard can devour you.
Schieffelin's yen—to shakespeare America's
forests; (thankfully, of the 60 birds alluded to,
more than half, ravens, loons, jays,

were already inhabitants).
After success with starlings and sparrows,
English sparrows, problems arose;
the 100 nightingales (14 citations)
and skylarks (20), were torn apart by hawks
before his eyes, one by one.
The woodcocks were knocked down
from their roosts in the lilacs,
by men who came to the park
at dusk, armed with long poles.
Likewise, the snipe (*Othello* I.iii; l. 233),
disappeared without a trace.

But, thick as birds in the text
of *A Midsummer Night's Dream,*
ousting native warblers from their nests,
the starlings and sparrows proliferate,
spreading like Shakespeare's words,
his c.1,760 coinings ready currency anywhere:
aerial, bump, dwindle, pedant,
barefaced, fretful, hint, lonely—
think of all the loneliness we'd never have known,
without *Hamlet* III.i; l. 45.

Like a modern-day Pandora, Eugene
releases more winged creatures:
magpies, cuckoos, ostriches, crossing names
off his list, his inner concordance;
taking the Bard's figures literally—
a parroting, a parody of pedantry
(the word *the* is used 27,457 times in the Plays).
Not "a swanlike end," "stalking like a peacock,"
"to seem a lapwing," but swan, peacock, lapwing.
In troops. Tropes become feathers and flesh.

By 1920, campaigns to eliminate *sturnus vulgaris*
underway in every state: nets, shotguns, clouds

of poison gas; glue slathered on railings and ledges.
With little success. Witness, these daily visitors
to my backyard, hustling the grass
with jerky, urban steps, mimicking the traffic—
horns, brakes, tire squeals, mimicking other birds,
power saws, each other—making so much noise
I can't hear my poem…
Last heard of Mr. Schieffelin,
he was holed up in his mansion,
chanting Shakespeare: "I took this lark for a bunting…
I know a hawk from a handsaw."
Daily harassed by stone-throwing crowds
who gathered at his gates;
he slips away from his estate, disguised
as a scarecrow, and sets off, incognito.

Lark

Before Earth (Aesop says)—just
larks.   And air.
Soaring, swooping,
riffing through the unruffled
nothingness.

Lark's father fell sick, and died; just
hanging there, day after day, mid-sky.
Without Earth, how do you hide the dead?
Let them rest?

On the sixth, Lark, half-
mad, perplexed—in reverence,
made his brain a nest,
he laid Dad down inside his head.

Poking out, in back, Pa's
claws itched a bit, but as he rose,
became defined: a crest. A badge,
which read: *Lark—the light-hearted.*
No obstacles. No strings attached.

A clean death, at last.
Far below, time for some dirt:
an egg-shaped clot
of mud and rock appears.

Catbird

Mole-colored, secretive,
its motto: "forever in thickets"
its cry: a catlike mew, but
muted, dubbed, dampened,
furred; hard to trace, as if thrown
from behind a wall, inside
a trunk, under the breath, kitty
caught down a well, what
the ghost of a cat might mutter.

Other birds keep away—
"mouthpiece of the enemy."
Even cats, drawn near
by its intermittent wry meow,
turn aside, saying, "oh,
that bird."

Dovetail

i.

For several years, more and
more mourning doves have appeared
in this widows' neighbourhood
softening the air with their feathery keening,
the heartbeat of their heathery wings.

So now, although the broken consonants
of starlings and grackles still tick and take off
the slow hours of the afternoon—
still call out the widows' names:
"Mrs Balch…Mrs Pritchard…
Mrs. Colson…Mrs. Pacey…"
at dawn, and twilight, murmur
vowels of grieving, their forever song:
"You…You; You…You."

ii.

A pair rises from the rowanberries
each evening as I walk
along the shining railway tracks;
disturbed from the bright red berries,
they yawl off in a circle
return to the bush when I've passed.

Always this pair;
me alone, thoughts of you.

Waxwing

They always pass through this time of year,
when haws and chokecherries are ripe;
small flocks stripping fruit
from the trees, passing it beak
to beak along the branches for
the last to eat, a trick picked up long ago
by fans at Fenway.
(And passed along, ballpark to ballpark.)

I always assumed you were named for Icarus,
the boy with wings of wax—
say, in a lesser-known version, he didn't drown, but
was spared just before striking the waves,
turned into a small brown bird. Sentenced
by the sun to endless earthbound flights
in search of food.
Reborn, like Halcyon and her husband
as kingfishers, or the sisters, Procne
and Philomela, as swallow and nightingale,
just before their cruel murder.
Eyes caught by the bright red drops
of wax on your wingtips, would recall your tale,
read a badge of lost pride.

So you fell a second time, when I found out your name
no allusion to the boy punished by Apollo;
but the colourful wax women used,
side by side dyeing clothes
hundreds of years ago,
when birds were given today's names.

Blake says everyone should determine
his own mythology,
"or be imprisoned by another man's."
Icarus didn't die; he was transformed into

a humble bird, hard wax stuck
to his wings, so he'd never again
fly too far from the earth;
he works his way forever north, pursuing
haws and cherries
a merciful sun slowly ripens.

Hummingbird

The Mayans say: God brooded
in his workshop, looking
down at his collection of birds:
the swimmers, runners, those that fly
high in the air, stay close to earth.
Some piece was missing, a small detail
before the set was complete.

From a heap of random sweepings,
he took milkweed down, seed pods,
filbert shells and dust;
not out of whole cloth, but from patches,
leftovers, scraps. Borrowed two drops
of pure energy, like honey, from
the sun; snagged a piece
of passing whirlwind
to fashion hinges for his wings.
A gob of pine tar for glue,
then he breathed on his dustball,
placing it, hovering, in the air.

Made a mate, and announced their wedding;
nuthatch functioned as priest.
Lark gave a wedding shawl woven
of cloud wisps;
to give their plumage iridescence,
burrowing owl gave the couple
jewels from under the earth.
Osprey gave a pair of pearls from the sea,
blackbird brought a bag of cherries.

A month of consummation for all earth,
of honey sipped from tall flowers.
Of hovering. A honeymoon
hot-blooded, hyperactive.

Ruined Gardens

A lawn unmown all summer—
even the median resembles a meadow
where a handful of sheep might pasture,
a harvest of timothy and clover;
a few flyers curling on the verandah.

Vancouver, Thunder Bay—I scout for clues
in likely neighbourhoods: a step
that needs mending, drawn blinds,
an odd light on all night—Fredericton,
Montreal—cats, patches of worn paint,
wildflowers taking over, an old one
continuing on inside; I'm drawn here
like a criminal, grail of late-night walks,
bike rides, detours. Chapels. Harbours.
Dropping by at odd hours
like a gardener performing his chores,
though I'm only here to cheer on the weeds,
pay homage to what's left.

Out back, crouching among the shrubbery,
by the hole in the fence, I kneel
in some native weed that
emits a rich odour when crushed—
a thick salve that's healing me.

Balsam Pot

Cleaning out Mom's cupboards,
come upon a battered pot
encrusted with yellowish residue
like dried mucilage, or mucous.
Before I can toss it in the toss-out box,
an aroma catches me;
I hold it close, and breathe.

On winter nights, wheezing
with a cold, my father would mix water
with spirit of balsam,
cook it up in this pot.
For hours, he'd sit bent over it
at the head of the table, kitchen
door closed, as clouds of steam and incense
anointed the house, a bath towel
shrouding his head like a swami's,
he'd stare into this enigmatic pot,
and breathe slowly in and out.

Like an oracle, waiting for messages
in the residue, waiting for relief,
he'd breathe slowly in
and out, the essence of fir needles
steeped, breathing again, giving him breath.
Nights forgotten, until this old pot
rimmed with residue, reminded me,
called them back.

Now when I walk beneath balsam firs,
a light rain, their scent descending,
clouds of my father's breath, finally
free, cling to me.

The Fatherland

It always rains here, constant, bone cold,
like rain in Normandy;
but this land's not the homeland,
Pacy sur Eure, a little town
where a great peace was signed,
close to a hill called the Somme
where my father's father died
without ever seeing his son.
My epitaph?   Pacey has his peace at last.

No, this land lies here inside;
night falls, and the rain begins again:
we walk beside a great river in flood
on separate peninsulas,
thin tongues of mud.
My father wears his old trench coat,
sometimes he stops to wave,
then goes on. He wants
to speak, but the water between us
is too wide and deep.

The Final Pages of Another Novel

It's late at night as I hit the final pages,—
my eyes flicking left to right and back—
boustrophedon—"turning the way oxen
turn in ploughing," faster now,
strands weaving together,
the inevitable twists,
a sense of harvest, and of winter,
momentousness on the way.

It was all uphill in the opening chapters
but momentum's downwards now:
faster and faster,
accelerating until the black particles
of each letter start to fly apart,
the sentences break down, disintegrate
and I stumble, have to reread each line,
each word imploding
like matter within a vacuum.

Then a tingling begins all over,
my arms become gooseflesh,
I shiver, look out the window
expecting to see snow,
look back at the page—the last
paragraph's gone white,
there's snow everywhere—
every novel should end with falling snow,
a white burst of light.

About the Author

Michael Pacey was born in 1952 in Fredericton. He received his BA and BEd from UNB, his MFA, MA and PhD (specializing in Canadian literature) from UBC. His work has appeared in more than twenty literary magazines including *The Malahat Review, The New Quarterly, Exile, Prairie Fire*, and *Descant*. He has also published a chapbook (*Anonymous Mesdemoiselles*, 1972), and a children's book (*The Birds of Christmas*, 1987). He was editor of *Prism International* and has taught at UBC and Lakehead University. This is his first full-length collection of poems.

Eco-Audit
Printing this book using Rolland Enviro 100 Book
instead of virgin fibres paper saved the following resources:

Trees	Solid Waste	Water	Air Emissions
1	71 kg	4,698 L	185 kg